Compliments of:

SHRINE & MUSEUM

601 North Townsend St. Syracuse, NY 13203

315.422.7999

SaintMarianneCope.org

Saint Marianne of Moloka'i

Heroic Woman of Hawai'i

Written by Mary Cabrini Durkin, OSU

Collaborator: Mary Laurence Hanley, OSF

Illustrations by Augusta Curreli

ÉDITIONS
DU SIGNE

Publisher:
Éditions du Signe
1 rue Alfred Kastler
CS 10094 – Eckbolsheim
67038 STRASBOURG CEDEX 2 - France
Tel.: **03 88 78 91 91**
Fax: 03 88 78 91 99
E-mail: info@editionsdusigne.fr
Web: www.editionsdusigne.fr

Written by:
Mary Cabrini Durkin O.S.U.
with the collaboration of: Mary Laurence Hanley, O.S.F.

Illustrations:
Augusta Curreli

Layout:
Éditions du Signe

2nd edition - 2012
ISBN: 2-87718-950-3

Printed in U.E.

Have you ever heard of the island of Moloka'i? Have you ever heard of the disease of leprosy? In this book you will learn about them.

You will also meet a little girl named Barbara Koob who grew up to become Mother Marianne Cope. Mother Marianne followed Jesus, who said, "Whatever you do for my littlest brothers and sisters, you are doing for me."

Moloka'i was on Mother Marianne's path to heaven.

A crisp snow lay over the village of Heppenheim in Germany on January 23, 1838.

4

But Eva, Leonhard, and Mathias Koob were not outside playing in the snow. "I'm so excited!" Eva said. She explained to little Mathias, "We have a new baby sister!"

The very next day, the Koob family went to St. Peter's Church for the new baby's baptism.

"What will you name the baby?" Father Spreng asked. Papa Peter Koob spoke up. "Her name will be Barbara," he said. "She will be named after her mama."

When little Barbara
was a year old, her mama
and papa had a serious
conversation. "The farm
where I work is very poor,"
Papa Peter told his wife.
"I'm worried that I can't provide
enough food for our children."
"Some of our neighbors have gone to America,"
Mama Barbara answered. "Maybe there will be better
jobs there and a good place for our family."

Soon the Koobs were on a big steamship, crossing the Atlantic Ocean. Leonhard pointed, "Look, there's a fish!"

"I like to feel the waves rolling the ship," Mathias said. Little Barbara just sat on her mother's lap. She didn't like all those bumpy waves.

Eva kept looking far away, saying, "I can't wait till we get to New York!"

The family grew in their new home in the city of Utica, New York. Peter worked hard. The family lived in a small house on Schuyler Street, near the Mohawk River. An enormous woolen factory was built across the street. The Koobs could always hear the machinery running. Their only playground was the street.

When Barbara started first grade, she had to learn English, since her family spoke German at home. She practiced saying "Thank you" instead of "Danke." She liked to learn new things.

First Communion and Confirmation Day at Utica's biggest church, St. John's, was a very happy day for 10-year-old Barbara. "Dear Jesus," she prayed, "thank you for coming to be with me. Thank you for your love."

Barbara became a beautiful teenager. When she graduated from her parish school, St. Joseph, she got a job in the factory, close to home, to help support her family. She and her brothers began to use a new spelling of their last name: Cope.

Something sad happened. Her dear brother Leonhard got very sick. Barbara helped mama take care of him, but Leonhard died at the age of 20. Then papa became sick, too. Barbara was her family's cheerful helper.

Meanwhile, a deep desire was growing in Barbara's heart. She sensed that Jesus was inviting her to belong to Him alone. And she wanted to work for God.

Barbara met Mother Bernardina and the other Sisters of St. Francis who were teaching in St. Joseph's parish school. They followed the example of St. Francis of Assisi, who had brought God's love and joy to people. Barbara talked with Mother Bernardina about becoming a sister. When Barbara was 24, her papa died. Mama no longer needed her help. Now, at last, she could become a sister.

"From now on, you will have a new name for your new life," Mother Antonia told her. "You will be called Sister Marianne." For a year Barbara wore the white veil of a novice, while Mother Antonia taught her about the life of a Sister of St. Francis.

Early one morning the new Sister Marianne and four other young women carried lighted candles into the Church of the Assumption. "I vow and promise to Almighty God. ..." Each one made a sacred promise to belong to God.

"As a sign of your love
for Jesus, here is a crucifix
which you will wear
all your life,"
Mother Antonia said,
placing the cord around
Sister Marianne's neck.

DEO

"Sister Marianne, please help me find the Pacific Ocean on this map," said a student.

"Yes, my dear, let's find it together." She was soon a teacher in Assumption parish school in Syracuse, New York. How she loved making the classroom beautiful for her dear pupils!

Meanwhile, there was no hospital in Syracuse, New York, until the Sisters of St. Francis started St. Joseph's Hospital. "Sister Marianne, we need you to get St. Joseph's Hospital off to a good start," she was told. Her heart went out to the sick people, who had no other place to go. She ran the hospital and also helped care for the patients. It was a big job, and she did it well!

"Sister Marianne is a good organizer," several of the sisters were saying to each other. "And she helps everyone cooperate cheerfully to do God's work," another replied.

The sisters elected Sister Marianne to be their Provincial Mother, the leader of the whole community. Now she was called Mother Marianne. She supervised the sisters in all the schools and hospitals and the building of a new chapel at St. Anthony Convent.

One day in 1883, Mother Marianne received a visit which would change her life. Father Leonor, a priest from Hawai'i, begged her, "Can you send sister nurses to Hawai'i? Many of our people suffer from the terrible disease of leprosy. There are no nurses to care for them."

Mother Marianne's heart was touched. She remembered that Jesus had cured people with leprosy, and that St. Francis had hugged a beggar who had the disease. She prayed for God's guidance. Then she and the other sisters agreed.

"Yes, Father Leonor, six volunteers will go, if we are needed so much. I will go with them to help them get started."

It was a long trip! They rode all the way from New York to San Francisco on a train. Then a steamship took them across half of the Pacific Ocean. Poor Mother Marianne! She was seasick the whole way!

KAUA'I

O'AHU

MOLOKA'I
Kalaupapa

MAUI

HAWAI'I

31

Hawai'i is a group of beautiful islands in the Pacific Ocean. At that time, it was not yet a part of the United States. It was a nation ruled by King Kālākaua and Queen Kapi'olani. The King and Queen and Mr. Walter Murray Gibson, who was the head of the board of health, had sent Father Leonor to find nurses.

When the sisters saw the leprosy hospital in Kaka'ako, an area along the seashore near Honolulu, they were shocked. There were rats and insects everywhere!

The superintendent was doing nothing at all for the patients. Soon the sisters had the place cleaned up and were putting bandages on the sores of the men, women, and children. For the first time, there were smiles on the patients' faces.

Now we have better medicines to treat leprosy, also known as Hansen's disease. But in the 1800s, the disease could not be controlled, and people thought that it was very contagious. Lumps and painful sores appeared on the skin and caused a bad odor. Eventually, most patients lost some of their fingers and toes, or even their noses. Everyone was very afraid of this disease, and people who had it were forced to leave home and live far from others. No one would touch them. But the sisters came to be their friends and care for them.

The Branch Hospital at Kaka'ako had a beautiful view of the ocean, but life was very hard for the patients. Some were angry with everyone, all the time. But that started to change when the sisters came. The queen noticed. She commented, "Mother, everyone loves you and the sisters, because you are so good to the patients."

When certain government officials tried to take advantage of the patients, Mother Marianne stood up for them.

"You have won our respect, Mother," Mr. Gibson said. "We will help you to make the hospital a better place."

"Well, Mr. Gibson, here is another need," Mother Marianne replied. "We must also help the dear children whose parents have leprosy. They have no home!"

"I will raise the money for these homeless little girls," Queen Kapiʻolani said eagerly. They all planned together, and soon a home was built, named Kapiʻolani Home after the good queen. On the day of the dedication, King Kālākaua honored Mother Marianne with a special medal for her goodness to the Hawaiian people. The sisters were the loving foster-mothers for the children in the home.

After some time in the Branch Hospital at Kaka'ako, Honolulu, the leprosy patients were sent far away to a peninsula named Kalaupapa, on Moloka'i. Moloka'i is another island of Hawai'i. Kalaupapa stretches out into the ocean and is cut off from the rest of Moloka'i by high, steep cliffs.

It is very hard for boats to land or to leave there. Leprosy patients lived in this isolated place till death. They had little or no health care. They could never leave Moloka'i, and few visitors were allowed. Their lives were sad, lonely, and painful.

In 1873, a young priest from Belgium, named Father Damien De Veuster, volunteered to be a chaplain for the lonely people of Moloka'i. He shared their hardships. He offered Mass and preached. He anointed the sick and got supplies for leprosy patients. He also built homes, laid waterpipes, and taught people to respect themselves and each other. He lifted the spirits of many and helped them prepare for death.

Father Damien caught leprosy too and suffered. "Take care of my boys," he begged Mother Marianne. After Father Damien died in 1889, Mother and the sisters took charge of his home for young boys with leprosy, helped by his assistant, Joseph Dutton.

Now Father Damien is called St. Damien, because he lived the words of Jesus, "There is no greater love than this, to lay down one's life for one's friends."

45

But how did Mother Marianne come to Moloka'i? Wasn't she planning to return home? Five years had passed since she left New York.

But so many people said, "Mother, we need you! Don't leave! How will the work for leprosy patients go on without you?" And so, in November 1888, Mother Marianne, Sister Leopoldina, and Sister Vincent made their home on Kalaupapa. Their small convent of St. Elizabeth sat on a windy, dry, bare patch of land, with the huge cliffs behind it, looking out to the sea.

Soon the sisters were busy taking care of many girls and young women who were being sent to Kalaupapa because they had leprosy. Usually, they had no friends or relatives to take care of them. Now they had a mother! The girls slept in little cottages with an older girl or woman to watch over them. They ate in a dining hall. Very sick people stayed in a nursing home. There was a fence around these buildings.

The whole group was called the Bishop Home after Mr. Charles Bishop, who had donated the money to build them.

Mother Marianne loved to make life brighter for the
girls. She sewed them clothes in the latest fashions
and taught them to make doll-dresses, press flowers,
and use sea shells in artistic designs. She and the other
sisters took the girls on picnics and played croquet
with them, or played the piano while they sang.

She protected them from all abuse and stood up for their rights and safety when officials or bad people tried to take advantage of them. Mother Marianne taught the girls to respect themselves and to make wise decisions.

All the while, she loved them and helped them to see how much God loved them, and that Jesus was close to them, even here on Kalaupapa, and even when they faced death.

Dry, dusty Kalaupapa began to bloom. "Mother, you've planted so many trees and flowers!" exclaimed Mrs. Kalani.

"Wouldn't you like to have some fruit?" Mother offered. She shared with everyone. "Oh thank you, Mother! Can you teach me to plant flowers, too?" "Of course! Then you will have your own beautiful garden," Mother replied.

No matter how many times a girl came to ask for a favor or advice, Mother Marianne always had time to talk with her children. Many a night she got up and went out into the darkness to tend to a sick person or to protect the girls from intruders. Even if some girls didn't cooperate, she would forgive them.

"She is a living saint," everyone agreed.

As the years passed, other sisters came to help. Life was not easy, but Mother Marianne kept up their spirits with her own cheerfulness and kindness. Every day, the beautiful and tender-hearted Sister Leopoldina bandaged the patients' sores. Sister Vincent and Sister Elizabeth did housework. Sister Crescentia and Sister Irene cared for the small boys at Kalawao, another part of the peninsula.

Dozens of Sisters of St. Francis have followed in their footsteps. None have ever gotten leprosy.

The Sisters of St. Francis helped many other people too. Soon after they arrived in Hawaiʻi, Mr. Gibson pointed out, "Mother, your sisters are needed in the town of Wailuku, on the island of Maui."

Facing another ocean trip, which always made her seasick, she and Sister Renata set out. Helped by the women of Maui, they opened Malulani Hospital. Sisters continued to serve the sick there until 1929. Today they continue to serve in other parts of Hawaiʻi.

Near the hospital, the sisters took charge of a school where a local woman was teaching. Mother placed Sister Antonella in charge. This was St. Anthony School for Girls, the first of many where the sisters would teach over the years.

How could Mother Marianne do so much for so many people? The secret lies in her heart, where she was always close to Jesus. She shared his love for people who suffer. Jesus said that when we help them, we are also helping him. God helped her to face suffering and loneliness with a smile. "Nobody knows but Jesus," she wrote in her diary.

She carried God with her through busy days and nights, whispering, "My God and my all!" Besides caring for the girls and tending the sick, planting and watering the garden, and keeping the chapel clean and decorated, she spent many hours writing business letters and ordering supplies.

As the years passed, Mother Marianne grew older, and her body became worn out by all the work she had done. She needed a wheelchair. Sister Leopoldina would push the chair onto the porch in the evenings, so that Mother could enjoy the cool air.

The girls of Bishop Home loved to gather close and talk with her. Sometimes the other sisters thought that she was too tired to have visitors. But she always said, "Of course, I want to see my children!"

One day, when she was too sick to come out, Teresa and Little Emma Kia sang a sweet duet outside her window.

On the morning of August 9, 1918, the sisters all realized that this would be Mother Marianne's last day on this earth. But she got up for meals, saying, "No tears!" Sister Leopoldina took her out on the porch one last time, and she waved lovingly to a little girl. That night the sisters gathered around her bed to pray. Quietly, Mother Marianne died, leaving this life on earth and beginning her life in heaven.

It seemed as though everyone in Kalaupapa who could walk came to the funeral in the Church of St. Francis. Then they walked in procession to a lovely spot among orange trees that Mother Marianne had planted.

There she was buried. Soon, the leprosy patients had collected enough money for a beautiful monument at the grave of their beloved Mother. It shows Jesus on his cross, reaching out to St. Francis.

Through the years since Mother Marianne lived on Moloka'i, many other Sisters of St. Francis have continued to love and to help people on Moloka'i and in all of Hawai'i. Some are nurses and have established more hospitals and hospices for the sick and dying. Others are teachers and guide young people to know, love, and serve God and to live with dignity in a spirit of service.

In fact, Sisters of St. Francis can be found in many other places in the United States, in addition to Hawai'i. Like Mother Marianne, they are doing God's work, in the spirit of St. Francis, cheerfully.

You can follow Mother Marianne's example by helping people who are suffering, sad, or lonely. That is how Jesus wants us to share his love.

Mother Marianne was officially declared a saint by the Catholic Church. She is now known as St. Marianne Cope. A shrine and museum honoring her are in Syracuse, New York.

You may want to say this prayer, joining other people who know how holy she was in her life on earth:

Prayer

Dear God,
thank you for helping St. Marianne
to be such a holy person.
Please guide me to follow Jesus,
loving others as she did.
May her example help
many more people
to make life brighter for those
who suffer.
Amen.

*If you would like to know more
about St. Marianne Cope,
or about the Sisters of St. Francis
of the Neumann Communities,
you can contact them at:*

**Sisters of St. Francis of the Neumann Communities
2500 Grant Boulevard, Suite 3
Syracuse, New York 13208-1797**

**www.saintmariannecope.org
www.sosf.org**